The Palace of O

PETER DAVIDSON was born in Scotland in ॰ sities of Cambridge and York. He was Wingate Foundation Scholar at the University of St Andrews from 1989 to 1990, and has taught at the Universities of Leiden and Warwick. Since 2000 he has been Professor of Renaissance Studies at the University of Aberdeen. His recent publications include *The Idea of North* (Reaktion, 2005) and *The Universal Baroque* (Manchester University Press, 2007). He was joint editor with Anne Sweeney of Robert Southwell's *Collected Poems*, published by Carcanet in 2007, and is a regular contributor to *PN Review*.

For Janey
Cor ad cor loquitur

PETER DAVIDSON

The Palace of Oblivion

CARCANET

First published in Great Britain in 2008 by
Carcanet Press Limited
Alliance House
Cross Street
Manchester M2 7AQ

A CIP catalogue record for this book is available from the British Library
ISBN 978 1 85754 926 3

The publisher acknowledges financial assistance from Arts Council England

ARTS COUNCIL
ENGLAND

Typeset by XL Publishing Services, Tiverton
Printed and bound in England by SRP Ltd, Exeter

Contents

THE PALACE OF OBLIVION

THE SPY'S LETTERS

ABERDEENSHIRE ELEGIES

Acknowledgements

My thanks to those who have read parts or the whole of this collection in draft: Pat Hanley, David Morley, Jane Griffiths, Peter Scupham, Margaret Steward, Jane Stevenson, Michael Hulse, Michael Bath, the late Anne Sweeney, Alison Shell, Arnold Hunt, Hugh Buchanan, Susan Bassnett, Andrew Biswell, Flavio Gregori, Ned Locke and Peter (*nihil quod tetegit non ornavit*) Blegvad. At the points where the text forced itself into a language other than English, I am grateful to those who helped to naturalise my rough drafts: Laura Tosi for Italian; Adriaan van der Weel for Dutch; Jane and Winifred Stevenson for Latin. I am much indebted for early encouragement to Alan and Susanna Powers, James Stourton and Oona and Brian Ivory, and to David Morley for making a context in which to continue. I owe Michael Schmidt and Judith Willson at Carcanet my thanks on many counts. *Stand* magazine published the first version of *The Spy's Letters*; *things* magazine 'The Englishman's Catechism'.

THE PALACE OF OBLIVION

Prologue: Speeches of the
Sovereign Lady Melancholia

Lady of cultured pearls, fictitious skies, real shit:
Stirring dust like powdered almonds, moving in sirocco and sacred
    heraldry,
Contriving aching magnificences, small acts of hysteria, under the
    landward wind;
I summon you my malcontents from ragged coasts, out of the vacuum of
    the burning afternoons
Lounging in silks slashed to tatters in guardrooms painted with the
    gorgon-breasted ancestors,
Practising imaginary marksmanship on the allegories of the ceiling; your
    arrows balanced with the feathers of swans and of the birds of New
    Spain.

Or drowsing on brocade imbrued with sweat and Sicily-water,
My tow-haired bishop's secretary, called by your fellows 'The
    Englishman' half in menace, half in jest
Chafing at having missed your appointment at 'The New World' brothel,
At whose head the ensanguined Saviour rears on the cross of cinnabar and
    silver
Rendering your nightmare back for your aureate dreams
– you are my man, come to me.

My keeper of the Duke's cabinet at the flea-bitten court in the mountains,
You who know well that delusion alone puts eloquence in the room of love,
Who have only silence in your heart, but speak out nonetheless;
The spiralling epigrams for festal days, *the contemplations of his serene
    highness in his courtship of the Holy Wisdom,*
The vertiginous odes wherein the company of the sky is summoned to
    attend upon his same three exiguous virtues:
As *the rose crowned with laurel, poetic applause* (your master having been
    chosen *gonfaloniere* for the seventh time)
Or *The Sacred Garland Restor'd* (his youngest daughter having entered the
    House of the Immaculate)
Mechanic of sacramental automata, librettist of sacred operas,
– come to me also.

I summon forth my malcontents from sullen fastnesses:
From the snow-leaguered cities, their fountains locked up in the frost,
Out of their muffled alleys and their night-moulded monsters of snow;

From the black manors folded in nooks of the hills,
Out of the lowering months of firelight, of the crystal retort, the silver tree
    in the chamber,
So my Narcissus of the Pennine tarn, so my Actaeon of the Bohemian
    forests.

And out of all places environed in dark, mordant waters,
Which turn to ice and stasis in the breath of the winter.
All states where the frozen canals glaze the stone treads of the water stairs.
Come, my Rotterdam Captain, from your saloons of green and silver
Where splinters of rain pit the surface of your mirrors, star your harbours.
You are mine, come to me also,
That we may celebrate the greater festivals of the Lady Melancholia,
I who am sovereign in this sublunar world.

All you who sleep amidst marble inlaid in marble until it has the fluency of
    damask,
Although there are towering plumes to the four golden posts of your bed,
Waking in the dark you see lost armies, crows following their pikes and
    their standards;
The end of Europe in sleet on a trampled plain; snow in infinity of
    muddied water.

The mirrors in the great room reflect when the chamber is empty
Of all save the wash of canal-light wavering on the ceiling,
These sleepless glories, weary pomps, the revels of Melancholia,
Those splendours which cannot staunch your impossible, twice-fallen state,
Nor can, nor will, heal nor reconcile you;
So that it will avail you nothing to exclaim:
'The Most Catholic Queen is become a golden palm tree.
And let this be set forth in hieroglyphicks by the *illuminati* of the English
    Province.'

I
Northern Casework

My taciturn masters to whom I send these dispatches:
Papers for the days of snow, italic winter trees;
Words for the months of rain, for the windscreen dashed silver, for
    storm-lit moorland patrols,
For the single light on the hill, for the steep road to the stone town off the
    wet fell;
Letters of late May, of elder bushes, of dog roses flourishing over
    blackened walls,
High summer reports of shirtsleeves and bright moors as far as the border –

I break my usual relation of villages guarded from intrusions,
    developments held at bay,
To write with all reticence gone, almost in fear, that the north grows
    strange, that my district is troubled about me,
And that these new encroachments lie in impalpable things.
I make my account, and lay my instances before you:

I adduce a tattered planning application nailed to a field-gate on Alston
    Moor: 'a plea for the erection of a cabinet of mirrors';
The raw new graffiti at Brampton quarry: 'Howle w^t. mee the Epicidium
    of the Queene of Arcadia'
And the gritstone house above Rookhope with the chronogram over the
    doorway
Has an addition to the inscription, which reads TERMINAT OMNIA TEMPUS
There was a date carved too, near to the date of this report,
But the cut stone flaked in the late rains and the ciphers are faint now;
In the loneliest field barn I found the remains of a playbill
*In this Seraphic Library the solemnities proper to the Academy will begin at
    their accustomed hour –*
And there was airborne dust, with a scent of powdered almonds, and a
    dubious sweetness in the air like muscatel.

The moorland church with a Roman milestone for altar,
Showed forth, when last I was there, a moment of intrusion:
It seemed for that second that great, dark canvases shouldered the chancel:
Marksman angels, cavalier in brocade, armed with matchlocks, seraphic
    arquebusiers –
But the semblances faded, leaving only grey stone in the last of the light,
Although when I left, the board outside had a torn notice beginning

The most secret opera of the Apotheosis and Consecration –
Too wearied, too sorry, to read it, with mist coming down, I stumbled
      back to the motor.

Most troubling of all, one winter afternoon, in light of Ravilious austerity,
I saw a fine, low-built house abandoned near the hill-road
And, the loose shutter yielding, a hasty flashlight inspection
Revealed an enfilade of rooms of recessive glory, painted in shell-gold and
      umber:
With ecstasies, torments, ascensions, their subject, apparently, *A Lament
      for the Jesuit Empires.*
And from the cellars the sound of water, as if lapping at ruins, fallen
      capitals, broken inscriptions.

Waking last night to damp westerly air, the autumn stirring my forelock,
I seem to glimpse the author of these invasions, my opposer in his regions
      of cordite and illusion,
Ill in a sullen manor amongst the canals and the weeping clay of the
      mourning counties,
Where the light has always the grainy quality of pre-war photographs.
He is dreaming of my grave north, my lead measures, my fells and riven
      stone.
I think I have sighted his agents, edging the crowds by the beastpens,
      flickering in ginnels –
As at Appleby, looking down on Boroughgate with the smoke low on the
      rooftops,
Or at the cross of Alston, light slanting over dark cobbles –
Their flaunting opposing our decorous colours of sorrow.

Lost at dawn or at twilight, I would confront him in his lands at the
      frontier of sleep,
If only he would dream himself within my reach –
That I might catch him unreflected by the sombre tarn;
Or come upon him, faltering shadowless in the lee of the gritstone walls;
Or lurking shadow in shadow at the grave portal of the lead-mine;
Then I could reason with him below my storm-shot trees,
That he bring his dreams and contrivings to an end,
That it is but sorry mastery to mess with fetches and revenants,
In territories of slate and lead; silver and gritstone, once my inheritance.

But there is no way to take him, my accustomed circuit is broken,
And I am out at all hours, now everything is altered,
Walking the frontiers, playing cat and mouse with his agents;
The Muses' delinquent loves, his hit-squads in these stammering dales.

II

The Paradise of Women

What does the Duchess scatter as she flies?
Silken auriculas, artificial snow.

And through which tissues does she soar?
Sapphire and *filemot*, clouded Arcadia.

Her aerial conveyance above the vale?
Caparisoned Pegasus, bedizened in scarlet.

The western sky the while displaying –
Glimmering cinnabar, flaking vermillion.

The time and season of her soaring?
Harvest evening still and August passing.

Who guards the pastorals of Derbyshire?
Chloris of Bolsover, Amaryllis of Hardwick.

Name the women of the castle garden.
Margaret, Lucy, Eaffery, Katherine.

Rehearse the distant cities of their saints.
Amelia, Augsburg, Ferrara, Alexandria.

Their gentle white animals.
Distant in avenues, flicker in shadows.

The mottoes and sentences of the collars?
The snows our castles and our rest.

And what does the fountain do the while?
Asperge in diamonds, lustrate in crystal.

So that the white hand of Mrs Behn –
Feathers in trailing the pluming water.

So that the hand of Mrs Phillips –
Sinks in soft moss at the lip of the runnel.

So that the hand of Mrs Hutchinson –
Entwines a shadow in a braid of water.

The matter of the elegies of Mrs Behn?
Sadness of travel: O distant, intricate London.

The burden of the song of Mrs Phillips?
Partings far into Wales: women taking sweet waters.

The complaint of Mrs Hutchinson?
Gardens laid waste: the just republic abandoned.

What shows then in latest day, and pencilling far?
Visions of battlements, terraces of evening.

Then what awaits, the August evening occluded?
Sleep and the falling flocks of the great trees.

The sentence inscribed to mark their departure?
She was called, in Arcadian speech, Lesbia Cidonia.

With what magnificence will they lie in state?
In ardent chapels, armorials of candles.

And how in time will their tombs be ennobled?
Sidereal catafalques with silks auroral.

And which blanched paradise to harbour them?
Eagle peaks, O moons on glaciers.

Their epicedia beginning?
Shepherds weep, kind nymphs delight no more…

The deploration of their mourners –
Faded August, lingering sunlight all shaded.

III

The Keeper of a Troubled House

They have been gone for a month and already I have had to cover the mirrors:
To counter the troubling of the steel glass, the figures stirring there faint
    as breath misted in frost,
Shadows scratched in light as diamond-point on Venice glass, as the
    pencilling ice on the windows
Of this cold house which is restless still, as if processions with lights and
    incense were passing in distant galleries,
In corridors which hold their echoes. Papery litanies. Invocations in
    secretive tongues of the dead,
Sound in the mirrors of the great room, as folds of vast curtains stir in
    currents of cold.

I never saw them, I have seen no more than a hand at the door of a carriage
As they left this place at the equinox to begin their long travels southward,
To exile beyond the seas, in the iniquitous kingdoms.
Their fame was infamous; their departure a day of rejoicing
And yet there is an order to what they have abandoned,
A succession of ambiguous wonders at evening, with the autumn wind rising:
Scented herbs stacked in great sheaves by the hearthstones,
Bright birds, glittering like the flaunting birds of New Spain, battering the
    windows,
And butterflies in chill empty rooms, clouds of ephemeral wings rising
    about me.

I do not think that they can have travelled yet far beyond the seas
I am certain that they have not yet passed to the south of the mountains –
I imagine them in the Spanish Netherlands, in the playhouse of the college
    of treason
I imagine in their hands the printed *Argumentum De Gemitu Columbae*
And Mary of Magdala weeps before painted splendours – the frontispiece
    painted with drops of blood in chains like pearls
The effusion of the affected heart, dissolution in tears, *necnon Aprilis
    lachrymae in oculis*
Then the banderole blazes in the occluded heavens, and now the floor of
    the stage is a torn map, the tattered shires of England.
The Magdalene has turned to a fountain, a weeping pillar of obsidian,
And blood pours from the mouths of the lions and slowly,
White-vested, pale, carrying palms, the players assemble
To sing the antiphon of the Innocents under the bloody rain.

It is my part to patrol the boundaries of their darkness,
To exercise vigilance at this sullen turn of the year,
As winter approaching turns tawny England black and green
And the day is not far off when I will wake in snow-light striking the ceiling,
Wake, as I have begun to, with their voices in my ears:
Murmuring litanies of the darkening season:
Crystal of amethyst, briar of snow, rose-ash and frost-flower;
Ice in the twilight, stillicide of rime, crystal of snowflakes;
Distillation of snow, Queen of Miraculous Snowfall.

As the year moves to dark the house discloses its dangers:
I mistrust the cabinet of books, the hexagonal mirror of silver,
As if the books, once read in the glass, will be filled with
Histories inverted, not all of them done with.

Chambers open in the depths of the mansion, full of things lost and
    abandoned
In the last closet, a painting of an Ethiop with a light burning in a red glass
    before it, a lamp which I cannot extinguish.
In the freezing room over the gate, the broken memory theatre, *This is the*
    house of Psyche and of Love;
Its pasteboard arcades marked with the names of the demons.

Now that it snows on their gardens, their mazes shift cut-works under the
    snow:
In the box parterre a lacerated heart, a heart aflame, forbidden hieroglyphics.
Which things were all hidden from sight until the first snowfall.

In the dawn, I wake to hail like chainshot battering the casement
Watching the ice-thorns, frost-needles form at the window,
Struggling free as they have drawn me to them in my dreams:
Feeling, in fear and attention, that I have wintered in their past
Where their carriages rattle to volleys of sugared almonds under the trees
    in the *corso*
And I have only my simple lucidity to oppose to their riches in darkness.

To the shadowed arcades where they linger to watch the approach of the
    evening,
With music playing not far off, courting the echo,
Foretelling, ravished, the end of all love and all pleasure:

Qual armonia celeste, qual aureo carmine?
Nemine.
Qual estasi vespertina, qual gioia della mattina?
Utinam.
Qual delizia mattutina, gioita nella sera?
Sero.
Chiarezza d'alba, perla di Parthenope –
Inopem.
Note di silenzi, chiarore nelle tenebre –
Tenebrae.

Under the loggia, to the silver of the harpsichord, the eunuch sings of
      translucent day, of the pearl of the siren of Naples,
And twilight draws forth the nymphs of Campania, descending with tapers
      from starry villages,
Down from the hills, out of distance and umber, as shadow falls from the
      mountain.

I do not know where they might be now, but imagine them always in
      shadows:
Recessive nights of the statued orange-groves
Or shuttered enfilades of pier-glasses and delusive skies.
The lead throws its reticulations onto this paper before me
And the earth in its iron furrows stretches away,
As I draw the shadowless light of midwinter England about me
My clarity, my own cold hardness in the eye of the frost.

IV
Apotheosis

The hangman's knife has forced the bud to bring the sanguine rose to
   birth.

Roping effusion of blood, centurion's scarlet, swathed over armour of gold,
Salmonic columns of jasper and lapis, emblems of constancy, emblems of
   strength and endurance.
Lasting pillars sustain them, silver arcades stretch beyond them,
Golden volutes uphold great works of touchstone and granite,
Whereon their thrones are set in perennial splendour.
Flames of marble, flames of Istrian stone, blaze at the mouths of the urns
   against the oriflamme of day
Blaze of the noon on white travertine, *pietra serena.*
Great banners crack open against azure, borne on Adriatic wind.

At Antwerp the burin scores their glories into plates of hammered bronze
Imposing the nimbus on their tortured brows:
The press at Rouen utters forth their wonders of endurance
Their seraphic contests of the block and the straw.
Their deaths are painted on the wall of the chapel at Rome
That all of faithful Europe may know this truth:
Who died in blood and straw now are exalted ineffable;
Their retinue the companies of stars of the heavens in harvest.
Who died at Tyburn and Lancaster are Dukes now in the empyrean,
And Princes in splendour bestride the skies of the morning.

But hear the ingemination of the dove:

Chorley mourns, Ormskirk is all forlorn,
Clitheroe and Crosby are undone.

Soft pacing, silver-footed, grieving from their springs
Ribble, Lune, Wyre and Mersey deplore them still.
Upland becks distil,
Springs on the fells arise in tears
Fill as crystal, well in their grief
To light, and fall to the dale.

Chorley mourns, Ormskirk is all forlorn,
Clitheroe and Crosby are undone.

Preston inconsolable, mourns through weeping October
The heavens revolve, grave Lancashire,
Weeps for them in the rains of December.
Which county has given the flower of her sons to the heavens,
Tutelars of lost manors, forgotten villages.

Chorley mourns, Ormskirk is all forlorn,
Clitheroe and Crosby are undone.

Transient armorials, trophies of rope and blade,
Blow in the coalsmoke above Burnley,
Wind-born heraldries in pewter skies,
Over secretive Towneley, amidst the drenched grass of the football grounds.

Chorley mourns, Ormskirk is all forlorn,
Clitheroe and Crosby are undone.

Weep, grieving rivers, mourning from your springs
Silver Lune, black Mersey, deplore them still,
Offer your tears to the seas, to the ebb-tide ever receding;
As drifting England mourns offshore,
Foundered in mist and schism still.

V

A Choice of Emblems

It is as though we were approaching the end of a fiction of espionage
Set in the last Edwardian years, amidst forebodings and rumours of invasion,
Greatly preoccupied with darkness and the sea, with docks, foreshores and
  saltings,
With wet steps leading down to black, uncertain waters,
With the loopholes where islands lie open to infiltration.

We may assume a pair of heroes of a familiar pattern;
Sporting undergraduates of impeccable background and set in their
  certainties;
So that their handsomeness and their obtuseness may equally be taken for
  granted,
As may their childhood years by the sea, in the south or the west of
  England,
In Lutyens houses full of shouting sons, with discreetly tended gardens of
  sea holly and lavender.

The greater part of the plot will be played out in winter in various
  obscurities of light:
Cambridge frozen at nightfall, London under the fog.
There will be infrequent gaslamps at corners, sudden torches in narrow
  places, gunfire and flares in the dark.

There may also be moments of arcane or magical significance:
Rooms of unimaginable, praeterite splendour in once fine houses deep in
  the London slums;
Music-halls, with light striking up from the pit on coarsely gilded pilasters,
And songs which lurch suddenly from innuendo into lucid, prescient
  despair;
And a master of spies, grinding the ash of a dead fire in his grey kid glove,
Then sifting it about him on the floor of a high cold room furnished only
  with umbered mirrors,
This last as a pantomime of warning to the two heroes, a reminder, which
  they do not heed, of their mortality.

The crisis takes place downriver of London, on remote mudflats,
Where they are awaiting the arrival of the enemy's emissary from the sea;
And have instructions that they are to kill him then and there, without
  weapons and without allowing him to speak.

After agonies of waiting, they hear a boat in the night, a step on sand, open
   their dark lantern;
And they both recognise their intended victim at that moment, each seeing
   the face of the other,
And in their moment of hesitation, he has time to escape again out to sea;
At which point they run, in blundering panic, uncertain of everything for
   the first time,
And run in effect out of the plot which first contained them and into a
   formless alternative;
Which finds them rowing the last of many twilight journeys towards an
   uncertain landfall,
Being set down from a coastal steamer on the northern shore of the Forth,
In the desolate coalsmoke and frost, the breath of Scotland in winter,
In obliterating greyness, in the dropping of day, red ploughland and wind-
   bitten trees.

They are entirely without purpose by now: squabbling, drifting from day
   to day,
Haunted by melancholy, their failure and the noise of the sea; seeing in
   everything on the shores about them
Only rot and tidewrack, the end of England.

It hardly matters to them that they reach a small town by the Firth,
And it barely strikes them that the place is deserted,
Despite coats of arms and datestones on the houses, suggesting that once
   this had been a place of consequence,
Despite a troubling inscription in Greek characters over a broken doorway,
   asserting that the Lord has provided and the Lord will provide,
Despite the slender market cross rising from the cobbles, the wind-wasted
   unicorn of Scotland crowning the shaft.
They pass down to the shore through the lightless town, to a straggle of
   vast houses facing into the noise of water.

In this way they arrive at the house that has been biding its time for them,
Fumbling with the unlocked door of the Palace of the Sandhaven,
A scraped match and a candle-stub their guide, they move through
   panelled or painted rooms
Crimson and lampblack shot with gold, in the last stages of sorrow and
   decay.
A staircase leads them up into the ribs of the house, the beams and spars
   under the roof,
And a last door from this emptiness into the boarded gallery.

Where the air is still and brooding and it is as though the room had been
    waiting for them
Through centuries of sea-mist and wind, of paint fading and flaking, until
    this sad, freezing night.
They have kindled a lantern now, and see that a barrel vault curves low
    above them and that it is painted with mysteries.
Blanched hyena-women point into landscapes behind them at enigmas and
    disasters –
Queens and sirens before shipwrecks, single combats and burning towns.
And each picture has a scroll above and a couplet painted below it.
Words deciphered in the unsteady light; forebodings and prophecies.

A winged book, the paint abraded to the wing-bones, hovers over a
    window, bearing a scroll lettered *invicta veritas*;
A woman with a mask of white lead sings a ship onto the reef, the words
    below *him self destroyes*;
A worn figure with a column and a palm-branch, the word *victoria* hanging
    in the dimness above her;
A faceless woman offers a flat drinking cup and the words below are *spoile
    and paine*;
Fortune smiles as a ship founders behind her, with the word, *declinant*;
In the corner of the ceiling is Secrecy herself with fast shut book and
    finger to her lips.

Obsessed in a moment, they light candle after candle as they try to
    decipher the ceiling,
Convinced that it must hold an answer for them, that it contains an
    explanation
Of their failure of nerve, and of the magical dangers which have bested
    them.
They cross and recross the gallery moving from picture to picture,
Their feet tracing patterns as intricate as those star maps fading in
    chambers below
(It is thus that the house accomplishes its purpose).
But it will neither yield to them, nor will it absolve them;
They roll themselves in their greatcoats and try, disconsolate, to sleep;

Out of the dark the prefiguring shadow and flare of the Grangemouth
    refinery
Flames, to their final despair, in the glory of a bombardment from far out
    at sea.

VI

Atalanta Fugiens

Instrumentum regni within the closed walls of the palace.
The troops of Spinola at every port of the city;
On the wall by the marsh-gate pasted this tattered paper:

QUAERENDUM,

Puer ingeniosus aptus ad basiliscibus futuere, desideratae lamiarum complere, mantichorasve irrumere, paratus in speculis spectare sine viso vultus suum; volens vigilare in limine stricto ense argento. Diligens lachrymas numerare animae mundi. Ut praemium erit cognoscere, anima amissa, carnem stellatum decanium planentae, viare invisibilis et libertus sicut corvus super urbes obsessas furcasque, sine vestigiis linquere in pulverem palatii memoriae, vivere in refrigerio inter solides geometrici, sine dolore ire inter ruinas Europae prismatibusque.

VII

Returning at Evening

It is as though we return at evening after a journey lasting months or years
(Approaching the gates of the park, mooring the boat at the water-stairs)
To find few works ruined and few things terribly altered,
But everything larger somehow and emptier: the distances further
    recessive, the groves more profound,
The balustrades softened with lichen. Cut walks and espaliers
Turned straitened avenues where low boughs brush the long grass of the
    rides.

But our ingenious conceits are gone: parterres of flaming hearts, of secret
    monograms and wounded eyes;
Salmonic columns, tuneable fountains, and poised spheres of crystal all
    broken,
Pavilions demolished which ciphered the courses of planets, whose
    geometries traced numbers of heaven.
In their place some coarse notion of beauty in deer-parks and groves;
And monstrous women of marble, not even able to speak;
With their names carved below them, *Respublica, Astrea, Justitia.*

Some things are strangely unaltered: *Atalanta Fugiens* lies open still,
On the figured table in the farthest banqueting house
(Open – incredible – at the plate showing the drowning of the son of the
    winter king,
As it was abandoned on the night of thunder, *accidie* and sudden
    departure).
But there is a soft layer of golden dust now over everything:
Motes stir in the light, the transient empires of the fall of the air
Are poised in their last suspension before the turn of the year.

In the house the glasses are shrouded, but, quickening to our voices, reveal
Our silvery voids, infinities of cloud, perspectives of obelisks and shadows.
Glimmering butterflies waver like fallen leaves in vacant passageways,
Mingling with the filaments of scented herbs, frost flowers, feathers of
    birds of New Spain.
Our lights, our quenchless lamps, shine unwavering as in Tullia's tomb,
But the wonderful pictures they honoured are lost to the blades and the
    flames.

Our books of secret histories, read by half-light in the octagonal mirror,
Retail once more the victories of Turnus, the abject death of Aeneas,
And Spain triumphant in the green waters off England.

The house breathes again as we pass into its recesses, into the closets and
    cabinets opening to receive us,
The cornice quickens as we brush it, flowering in immortelles, in
    Melancholia's hellebores;
The windows shine with the diamond-hieroglyphs tracing their quarries;
The doors have their watchwords, again all the house fills with whispers
    and eloquent movements of breath.

In the park, the great trees hold their leaves, although past the arches and
    terraces
Are the washes and wastes of Naples-yellow air,
Insinuating cold for all the late warmth of the sun.
And evening has come and no doubt of the autumn tomorrow,
The summer's lamentable end in smoke and the harvest;
The last days before the freezing distillation at dawn and the umbering
    wash on the plane trees,
And ripeness gone over into desolation: it is so far to the north here,
It is as if we were in England and looking down in unforgiving wind on
    reaped fields, tawny horizons.
(How little our silks avail against this chill, this September air,
against the numberless, unhappy rumours in the wind.)

Tonight we cannot rest; we must walk to the furthest reach of the park
And twilight comes down with most of the ground still untravelled
Where half-remembered statues hold flambeaux in the depths of the
    leaves, statues with fires behind their eyes.

In this hour of visitations, troubled with glimpses and warnings
The distances constellate in light, beyond the flares of the bridges
And all the avenues end in wastes of darkening water:
Lakes and Lethean meres, sluggish impossible rivers
Beyond which foreshadowings stir as incandescent cities,
Reflected furnaces, towers of combustion, thunder in burning air,
Obelisks of lightning, castles of scarlet and flame.

VIII
Lamentatio umbraticolarum Pastorum de morte Reginae Arcadiae

Lugete pastores, plangite nymphas
Mortua, heu, moestissimae Regina Arcadiae.

Cyprum tollite platearum, myrtum montium:
Siptachorae lacriment electrum, margaritas nebulae,
Imbres venerunt, mox pruinae sequentur.

Lugete pastores, plangite nymphas
Mortua, heu, moestissimae Regina Arcadiae.

Imbres venerunt, mox pruinae sequentur
Ubi fragae dulces olim, sunt spini amari fimbriae,
Capitaque arborum inclinata adhuc canescunt.

Lugete pastores, plangite nymphas
Mortua, heu, moestissimae Regina Arcadiae.

Et capita arborum inclinata adhuc canescunt
Imbres venerunt, mox pruinae sequentur
Regnum sero apricum, felix olim, luctans quoinde.

Lugete pastores, plangite nymphas
Mortua, heu, moestissimae Regina Arcadiae.

Regnum sero apricum, felix olim, luctans quoinde
Festa praeterita, deliciarum finis veniet,
Cunctas felicitates offerimus ad pyram reginae.

Lugete pastores, plangite nymphas
Mortua, heu, moestissimae Regina Arcadiae.

Cunctas felicitates offerimus ad pyram reginae.
Serta, personae, flabella, larvae, unguentes
Sericae argenta flores cordaque crystallina.

Lugete pastores, plangite nymphas
Mortua, heu, moestissimae Regina Arcadiae.

Sericae argenta flores cordaque crystallina
Chirothecae daedalae, aromatizantes manicae
Floribundae, ut horti olim devastati nostri.

Lugete pastores, plangite nymphas
Mortua, heu, moestissimae Regina Arcadiae.

Floribundae, ut horti olim devastati nostri
Imbres lutulant canales, fontes frigescent
Busta cadent, membra superstrata rubis.

Lugete pastores, plangite nymphas
Mortua, heu, moestissimae Regina Arcadiae.

Busta cadent, membra superstrata rubis
Rosae spineolis revertent malis cydoniae
Nemora concrescunt densam in silvam.

Lugete pastores, plangite nymphas
Mortua, heu, moestissimae Regina Arcadiae.

Nemora concrescunt densam in silvam
Ubi struimus famae trophaeum reginae
Ut hoc alabastron semper adornatum
Myrto montium, plataearum cypro.

IX
The Praise of the Winter

Shards of feather, dust of water, frost-down, powder of ashes,
Strow your benedictions of oblivion and cold.

There was to have been a water organ below the great parterre,
Abandoned in all its tones: Diatonic, Enharmonic and Chromatic all
    reduced to silence;
The grotto of the Aurora of the northern sky also fallen,
All glories aborted because of the wars of Bohemia.

Urania's sceptre, her fieldmarshal's baton of lead, is frozen, cracked by
    the cold,
The dials of the castle garden are broken and dark now.
The head of sentient steel and eloquent bronze is constricted to silence
    in starveling air,
Moist obelisks of glass are shattered to fragments,
And frost powders the gravel of the great garden, dust which is stirred
    with the first snow.
The feathers of snow light on the terraces, on blanched marbles, on
    black touchstone of Namur,
Which snow turns dun in muddied waters: Danube, Vltava, marshes of
    the mouth of the Rhine,
Snows lost in the sea-fogs over star-towns, dunes and the last islands.

Shards of feather, dust of water, frost-down, powder of ashes,
Strow your benedictions of oblivion and cold.

Fine towns are abandoned on plains of the Empire, the burghs usurped
    and every city is shaken:
Their fountains in ice are the tears of Europa these thirty murderous
    seasons:
Still winter's fountain's marble frozen, stillicide their murmur falling.
Prague, Heidelberg, Culross and Antwerp, all slighted and plundered,
Their squares levelled with snow are the pages whereon I inscribe this
    sorrowful history.

Which ends in the houses of the Count of Holland in his town by the
    marshes,
By the shifting dunes and sea-beaches which bound the beleaguered
    lowlands,

Where the widowed bed of the Queen is boundless and cold as
    Bohemia:
Her swans in frozen air will never fly now to England.

Shards of feather, dust of water, frost-down, powder of ashes,
Strow your benedictions of oblivion and cold.

Hague, place of exile, austerity, gravest exactitude,
Refuge, seat of the just and fragile republic,
The tentative starting-again of lachrymose, wounded Europa:
At your heart is the frozen lake: ice-black mirror of justice,
There are figures fashioned from snow in your squares, fugitive
    emblems of mercy;
Astrea, *Justitia*, patrons of hope and perseverance,
Semblances made in the night which will dwindle away with the
    morning,
Glazing your black court lake with blacker ripples of water.

Shards of feather, dust of water, frost-down, powder of ashes,
Strow your benedictions of oblivion and cold.

Marshes stretching away, chill groves, wooden farmtowns,
Towers in the frost; stark, filigree castles
Amidst infinite snowy parterres, their mists lifting at dawn.
The air occluded with flakes, as glass abraded in water.
Endless as exile, as far as the sea-voyage to England,
And glorying above, the crown of the north
And the changeable lights in its skies.

Words pass to echoes, lost in rumours of music
Sung in the icy streets, ballads of wars in the Empire,
Alva's myrmidons routed, with all the winged myriads of Spain:
Rhetoric and *History* sing from the scaffold in freezing dusk, tar-barrels
    lighting the pageant.

The Paltzgrave's black armour reflects this light of the north,
Here on his catafalque, in the embrace of the cold:
Amidst the crimson brocade, starred with the feathers of snow.
In her snow-cold arms, as if half-awake he was lying
In the arms of his wintery lover, in cerements of snow,
Fading with the flocks in the darkness, under sanguine and crimson at
    last.

And in the arches below the bridges, the beggars took up their song. They were the army of reason, marching by night, starving at the doors of reasonableness.

Ons erfdeel geeft ons sneeuw en ijs.
Zo kort voor ons het Paradijs

Kort het licht dat de zomer bracht:
Nu heerst winter en de nacht.

Zo betalen wij de prijs
Voor de vrucht in 't paradijs.

Sneeuw en ijs en doornenkroon –
Voorbeschikt voor ons tot loon.

Wij ondergaan dit zonder rouw:
God zij geloofd voor deze kou.

X

The Palace of Oblivion

Air like bottle glass, reek of elder, sky gone almost to nothing,
Dust, brash and coal waste on the dulled wash of the tide.
Northern summer afternoon under thunder unbroken
On marsh, foreshore, salting, waste. Sour water
Laps at the black foundations of the castle of unmaking –
Great pillars, work of giants, cyclopean walls –
Place of dust and palace of silence, salt lagoon where all endeavour ends,
Light roping into oily water, dying in darkening glasses.
(Exhaustion is but the first condition of reaching this place.)

This place of forgetting, death of the dust of memory,
Lost recollection locked in the choking rooms;
Snuff of candles, golden powder of laurels, cerements of silk-thread
In the shrouding, fading, closing, settling of dust thick as fur,
Under glassy air, and the storm (never in this region of inertia) breaking.
Why have you brought me to this shifting place?

Room after room, shut, locked and extinguished:
Corded bundles, shrouds, closed cabinets and chambers,
Barred shutters over ox-eye windows, nor moving, nor waking.
Sleep and slow and end and drowse and never.
Close darkness, whispering of dust, silence of water,
Blood, dust and dormice, revenants, shadows.
All gone and spent, quenched and forgotten now?

Mummia rotted to dust in the grotto, brick dust and weeds of the fabulous
     gardens, golden dust, Naples-yellow dust from desiccated laurels.
Time turns to powder, glory to touchwood, to coal dust on the face of the
     water.
Lit by torch or candle flame, scraped match or tinder.
The sluggish water washes the inscription in the cellarage,
Foundation of the palace of forgetting –

> WORLD OF LIGHT AND LEARNING BE UNDONE
> LOCK EVERY CLOSET OF THE TOWERS OF REASON
> CLOSE AND QUENCH AND FINISH AND FORGET

The air is foul and drowsy: for the dark, for melancholia, for secrecy.
For the saltings and the marshes, for oblivion and the ashes.
Coal dust water, air like glass, shadows, dormice, blood, dust, dreams.

And is there anything to stay us here?

Epilogue: Recitative and Aria of the
Sovereign Lady Melancholia

Stay for me, my only love, my hierophant, my despairer,
Where you watch at the last reach and wash of the lagoon, far past the
    casino of the spirits
In the black loneliness of your saltings, below the cerements of evening,
    under clouds blowing smoke-grey and sulphur,
Your tower of the orders of twilight, architecture of regret and departure.

You linger by the dry cistern, the lizard-basking cistern
To rehearse your eschatologies, whisper your sibylline verses,
To scry in the brackish mirror of your saltmarsh pools
For the trail of phosphorescence defining the form of the eidolon,
For glassy visitants, lucent messengers, whisperers of passwords,
    conspiracies, disasters:
The rosy cross, the finish of all sublunar things, senescence of the world.
Shrieks, murmurings of distances, chances missed,
Lost origins, umbrage, disasters, copulations with ghosts.

O my *impresa* is a field of fallen snow
Grazed by the white stag, the maculate unicorn, attended by the raven:
And the sentence of Melancholia was ever *Life is Long*.

Consider but the ends of my lost darlings:
The great instauration dwindled to a club of the disaffected in a garret by
    the marsh-gate;
The apric empire perished in thirst and fraught with fevers:
Finding no ore in the dusts of the Indies, but only the apple of lead.
The western design foundered in straits and the shallows,
Lost off Hispaniola, killed from the shadows, driven back to the ships,
Dead of delirium and their endless journey, destroyed by thirst and the sun,
And yet grandiloquent in their last extremity:
Our names not unworthy to stand with those of the ancient heroes.

And think on the books which will never be finished: the lives wracked in
    fragments:
As *The Epithalamium at Cuzco for Doña Beatriz Ñusta and Don Martín de
    Loyola*;
The folio of the adamantine tempests in the Gulfs of Venice;
Abandoned pamphlets, disbound: *A letter concerning Bloud and Things
    Strangled*;
Torn papers of cosmologies, *The Posthumous Traveller*.

Aching always for the shadow of your face,
Searching every flaw and facet of my rose-cut diamonds for its refraction,
As twilight dims my windows, and my grandeurs debar me from love,
I scan every casement for your reflection, all night through,
(My glow-worm taper quickening the feathery dark of the great villa)
Until the first light's despair and the stifled day:
My airless gardens abraded as the park of the Bel Respiro,
Dusty canals, abandoned groves, malarial splendours at noon,
Desiccate moss on my statues, my islands lying far under heat beyond reach.

Attend me at the sea-gate of ivory, master of my barque *Disquietude*, riding
    at wharf on black water.
Attend me with sheet lightning, muted trumpets, summer thunder,
    mourning sails,
Under involutions of light, roping of rose-gold and umber,
Launch my triumphal progress of sorrow over the lagoon at evening;
Until my black swan's wings draw down the dark,
Until my sable fireworks blaze their blackness in the midnight skies.

My love and grief, I have watched you in glasses all day
Knowing this, your most secret movements have a conscious grace, an
    unnatural elegance;
At the last obscurity of cobalt dusk you will hear me
Singing in obsidian and out of standing pools,
Singing from mirrors of black water, whence my shows have dimmed and
    departed,
Relinquished to the passage and flow and wash of the watery light.

Howling forth my regrets in orchidaceous Latin,
Parching and starving amidst the chambers of marvels,
Mourning in diamonds and tissue of silver, in coloratura of sorrow
I sing my age of gilded iron to rest.

Aria

Blow the sea to frost and glass
freeze and still the springs in ice

Rain on the far marches, dust
and silt remain of all the past

Desolate, elegant, the lost
frontier captain holds the waste

deserts of mist, chasms of sand
I am come to lock all fast

THE SPY'S LETTERS

for AHvdW

I

And how would you suggest that I should live in England in this year
– and how should anyone live in England now?
(We raised our eyes from the systematic gardens, the classical villas, our
    black, encompassing water.)
As a spy. How else?
But how should I begin to think of it?
Especially where speech and writing are proscribed?
With invocation of rain, in fear of the Muses: the usual precautions.

II

Why is it raining always in cities of exile, in sympathetic deploration,
    sorrow's literal rain?
In this country they have an evening hymn, which commends
Their ship canals, their houses of brick and Portland stone
To the reasonable God, who tinted the lemon-yellow of their sky –
Conversely, the tattered theatricalities of their urban evenings,
Greasepaint, jellies blurring behind mirrored blocks and steeples –
Argue less powerfully for a God of reason, or reasonableness.

The rain in the cities of exile lacks the quality of that rain
Descending with the distillation of willow leaves
(My love, to whom I send these dispatches) which is gentle upon your
    willow gardens.

I send this thinking of the formal canals of your gardens,
Urns on the twin bridges, distances of mist, waters joining and parting.

III

The three seaward walls have their nightnames still: *maker, sleeper, dreamer.*
I whisper your titles when I'm half awake: those deriving from the saltmarsh
and the linden tree (where they said that the apparition was seen by half the
children of the village); the names deriving from the shelving bed of the river,
from intricacies of water; the outlandish honorific conferred by the fugitive
scholars when the City fell, and the appended names of your fortress-towns
(my love) like stars with their gibbets looking seaward by the water-gate.

IV

Fear wakes me earlier, smoking in the half-light, listening for dawn,
If I am less *here* than in a future *there*,
Who keeps the Palaces of Recollection?
When *here* is only absence, fugitive, unstable history under the hand,
The place I come from recedes from me.
Could I return, if they recalled me, those who keep the Theatre of Memory?
I have forgotten sleep, and grow oblivious in obedience.
Light, and the joiner whistling to work, the car from the lane end on the
    school round.

O there in gravity, in sorrow here, our heraldry is distance and the weather;
By its European river, and of its mist the essence, who now keeps the
    Palaces of Memory?
Dawn in rain and sorrow of willows lifting and dropping
In deplorable late September, rain of exile,
As the geese pass over, weeping.
As the swans pass over, crying.

V

I travelled here from London on a train
Which turned and burrowed inland, far from sea.
In doing this I followed my old orders
Which lead to the dead centre of this country.
Imprisoned by the falling of the evening
My time is dusk and tedium and rain.
Downwind the grass smells strong here after rain.
The wires still hum after the long passed train;
My time is dusk and tedium and evening
Looking across the shifting inland sea
Of grass, which is the heartland of this country,
The place where I am held by secret orders.
Waiting in vain, being landlocked without orders,
Drowning in absence like the driving rain
Remembering my lost and misted country,
Memory brings new sorrow in its train:
O war, o war ich jenseits der Wellen,
Im scheidenden Strahl des Abends.

Rain and the dark and boredom fill my evening
I scan the last encodement of my orders:
Love and his train in order passed the seas
Leaving an emptied country, evening rain.
Approaching night, the whistle of the train
Brings dusk and tedium to fill this country.
Looking too lonely in this rainy country
The doctor's wife looks out into the evening
Half listening for the murmur of the trains
Which mark the hours with passing in their orders
She's by the window, looking at the rain
Falling on clay, as if she looked to sea.
I dreamed that this country lay below the sea,
That the green waters overwhelmed this country,
I wake to the soft attrition of the rain
Which falls in dark and boredom until evening.
I am obedient to my ancient orders,
I time the dead hours passing by the train,
And waiting in this country every evening
I learn that rain cannot unsalt the sea,
And train for action, but receive no orders.

VI

My principals are dead or have run mad through the ruins of their mirrored offices. Instructions in clear, on a picture postcard of the Casino Gardens, in a hand eloquent of the *ancien régime* and the Old Days at the Villa: *Report as a priority on the movement of clouds, on the flight of birds. If time permits, trace the courses of those rivers which lave the industrial centres.* Purple ink. Screaming. I ask you.

VII

Bones for the lottery: town ends, allotments, scrubland beloved of suburban murderers; black sacks and bones behind the hedge of the layby; watering can and pruning knife, heraldry of lost summer; sea willow, silver poplar, artemisia, burnet rose, the genteel plant called Miss Willmott's Ghost.

VIII

And which of you would *not* take flight, receiving, by the early post, a postcard in clear, in green ink, reading *Fly, all is discovered*?

IX

Delayed by the umbering of the avenues in the gardens of the Duc d'Enghien
Observing the withering hornbeams of the *grands berceaux*
And the brickpaved streets so trim, the coffee at the hotel so delectable,
    the sun warm at noon,
Time so deceptive: mountains in sight, the southbound trains so
    dependable;
And plane trees are such hysterics, faltering first, lacking all courage,
In the water-towns, amidst the ruins of the Palatine Gardens, I was slow,
    too slow to move southwards,
as the dark followed us on the rivers, closing after the Rhine voyage.

Passing too slowly southwards from safe house to safe house, the stuccoed
    classical villas,
At evening pianos lamenting with rain at the windows:
A succession of small apocalypses for those territories which with every
    cough I relinquish.

In the cold season of the Holy Souls, autumn took my throat in Germany
But granted one moment of vision: the walled garden of the merchant's
    house,
A cast lead cherub where paths cross, fallen leaves, it was wild, it was the
    end of Europe in little,
And they told me that there were mists and horn calls in the hills that day.

That evening seated at the birchwood bureau, with the green-shaded lamp
And with just the right level of wind laying siege to the house
(An 1810, a fortepiano wind)
I wrote the last letter to the one whose ancestry and titles composed the
    geography of my sombre childhood.
– violet stormclouds, combustion of the opera house, overdoses and the end –
This kind of thing is called either hysteria or the baroque depending on
    your own position
And takes more love, more discretion, than you might imagine,
When the address is lost and all the envelope's direction
Is to the site of the palace of recollection, sometime the theatre of memory,
The place where once a river, misted always, washed rostral columns and
    the prow of a galley in stone.

And suddenly the passes closed, the tracks impassable, hound-weather,
A little snow on the frozen rails of deserted stations:

That I may learn of the bloodied swan, of the wounded unicorn,
To make my utmost music for my destroyers.

And thus, at length, I have arrived by the carriageway of twilight in the
    coach of black water
At length I arrived at this place, whence I shall go no further,
Imprisoned as I am by frequencies of crystal, by swan-lustres of
    chandeliers and refracted snow.

Entering the blanched court chapel with its icy trees, the silver basilica,
Leaning on the cane of unicorn's horn mounted in silver;
I will end and exhale in plumes and towers of scarlet and silver,
Silver my spiralling breath, misted cinnabar and crimson.

Under the vaults they are singing of the midnight rose:
My breath has gone forth now a Jesse tree of air
I have flowered in the lacerations of the cold
My voice flows into the unstaunched wounds of the rose,
Their institution of eternal frost.

The Englishman's Catechism

for AARP

And what does the mirror show you?
Pale self, tweed coat, half-light, stillicide.

Where does the mirror hang?
Contrejour, tall windows, between dark and waking.

Beyond the windows?
Grass walks, ice house, yew henge, frost pavilion.

What lights your travels?
Gas lamp, oil light, headlamps, silence.

Describe your ideal divisional officer.
Midwinter, insomniac, baroque, time-bomb.

Permitted colours of dress on duty?
Ploughland, saltmarsh, tidewrack, claret.

Your sacred plants?
Wallflower, potato, leek, sweet william.

Correlatives of innocence?
Rag rug, auricula, brick path, cold frame.

Materiality of Paradise?
Millstone grit, ashlar, cobble, brick.

Safe houses?
Lock cottage, railway cottage, terrace house, hill farm.

Showings-forth. One example only.
Dog days, saltmarsh, drifting boat, garlanded.

Consider qualities of air.
Flint, turning, softening, stasis.

Speak to qualities of water.
Canal, fen-mist, fall plume, lake glass.

Minute operations of the rain.
Wet stone, wood drip, sea blur, bright lane.

Your theology?
Expiation, unfashionable things, passing things, caducity.

The cost?
Sorrow, loneliness, hurt in devotion, this dying island.

Your passport for the Gates?
No. Hush, caution, echoland.

And how might you envisage your own death?
Far provinces, small rain, October dusk, last love.

Portraits from the Thirties

for AMB

Long overcoat slung over his sanguine rugby shirt as he stands on the pavilion balcony, caught breath clouding about him. Pitch frozen now, goal posts overwhelmed in fog and winter. Clatter of cycles, boot nails on concrete, shouts fainter, going. Cold, streetlight, going.

He walks over cobbles out onto the fell above the town. Noises of trams below him, of the Saturday market. Thin sun slicing the fine ridge of the moors, last snow lying in the lees of the walls. Smoke rising in a wonder of air which is farthest and clearest west this fair morning.

Grey-shirted he cycles the road below the sea wall, far into Lincolnshire. Brick houses along the canal, seed packet flowers, fences and window-frames maroon and pea green. Strong tea from a battered metal teapot, hot afternoon motionless on cuts and long levels.

My father leans on the doorcase in his twentieth year, cooling sunlight throws shadows of windows onto white panels behind him. The guns are out on the hills now, the stags come down before daybreak to the windows of the lodges. Perthshire falters, is still, falters under the rising last-of-August wind.

ABERDEENSHIRE ELEGIES

I

Amor Patriae

Epistle to CDR

Smoke over conifers, rumours of snow in October,
Corgarff under frost; the Spey running broad over stone
(The rowans going over to gold, the first larch branches tarnishing)
Last slant of summer now passing, now past, in reaped meadows under
    our towers.

Soft dust on the fields now, showing white towards harvest,
Haar over barley, days closing in, summer boats anchored in harbour,
Leaving us lonely below cloud roads of flocks moving southwards
Awaiting the first real breath of cold from the mountains,
Alone with our north, husbanding this difficult land.

Austere virtuosi of absences, distance, occlusions,
Collectors of outland colours: dun, bistre, gradations of grey,
Salt-scatter of snow on the marl and ash of the ploughlands.
Bare trees lustred only at sunset in scarlet, frost-sapphire and azure –
The west limned with glimpses into bright realms in the hills.

Connoisseurs too of the north in its sombre closet of wonders:
Latin scratched on glass against low, early-westering light,
Treason glasses blowing lost midwinter roses,
Glass negatives of spires misted by time and winter,
The ivory spiral keeping the door of the chamber of twilight and ice.

So we look down from the Shiprow to icebreakers waiting their hours of
    departure
For norths barely imagined: white drift in brilliant night.
And think on our frontier dukedom, rubble altars marking the bounds of
    Empire.
Last, remotest throw of the Romans: cold cairns on the horns of Ross,
Stone portals of absolute north, farthest obelisks of snow.

II
Raeburn's Yellow

First elegy: to MFE

Inheritors of rain, peat-reek, titular baronies.
Under the storm forcing the dark north on the Garioch.
Waves break on gable-ends, rake the vennels at Crovie,
Buchan lies low, farmtowns in straining trees, doubled by force of the gale.

In this high, silent room smelling of woodsmoke, tobacco,
The only things moving the fire and the flame of the candle,
The troubled night and the gale a murmur, no more, in the chimney.
We talk late under the vaults shaped by Conn of Auchry
(Lion Rampant, arms of the Barclays, Passion Shield over the oratory),
Shadowed French portraits above us – monarchs, pretenders –
It is good to know where you are, wherever that may be.

We hunt the name of the colour that shades Raeburn's winter horizon,
Denser than north light caught in a glass of white Burgundy,
Apricot pale against snow clouds at sombre afternoon's ending,
Nor white nor yellow, whiter than chamois leather,
If we could but name it, we would hold the key of the winter,
The cold of late journeys from Edinburgh, light going over stations.

We tally the loss in this north where we rebuilt our houses:
Snow Kirk down and Snow Tower broken,
Tonley lost, Fetternear blinded, Huntly abandoned,
Storm over Gight and Strathdon – only the long songs remaining:
The travellers moving away from us through September berryfields,
Away in the dazzle of cold sun, over the frozen roads.
Those who know by words handed down which order the houses were
        searched
On the day when the redcoats came for Forbes of Pitsligo.

Logs waste and fall in the grate, the candle flame stammers,
And we sit late here tonight, holding in memory,
Gordons and Ogilvies, gone abroad, lost in the wars.

Settled and fixed in these regions of storm and felicity,
Having no longing to swell the crowds to the south,
Nor cross the ocean westwards, that Hesperia's spoiled.

III

Concerning Stillness and Distance

Epistle to RGM

This is the evening Scotland dreamed in exile:
October clouds, hill shadows, lucid smoke
Moving on slopes below. Sanguine and grey
The mountains and the sunlight hold the west:
The Cairngorms, with Torridon beyond.

I think you make such distances your own,
Your far dispatches bring remoteness near:
Climbing to silence, the loud scree beneath,
And stillness of the granite tops beyond;
Keeping the temporalities of snow
On silent margins of the frozen tarns.

Your quiet reports of summer progresses:
Fathoming gulfs of leaves in western shires,
The elder overhanging the green water,
Verdure redoubled, liquid depths of light.

This autumn you have travelled further still –
Parting with summer, wintering out the year,
So it takes maps and atlases to trace
Your far asperities of wastes and ranges,
And on you travel whilst I barely stir.
Head-down, below the snowline, keep the house,
Setting my mind to correspondences.

Letters grow almost voices at this season,
These words compose a fragment of our long
Conversation in the rooms of autumn –
Remoteness, woodsmoke, stillness, distances.

The sun's gone in: leaves litter the pathways,
The broken ash-frails drift on the upland wind,
Fret in our gravel alleys, pass and fall
To overlay the symmetries of gardens.

IV

The Apotheosis of James Byres of Tonley

Epistle to MEAG

Exile and return and bitching and fear and magnificence –
Launching Miss Fraser forth in death in her great barque of stone.

Applaud his return from Rome (gulf of antiquity, palace of shadows),
Gather about him the pale *accademia* of the white nights at high summer
Lit by the midnight dawn, bearing torches and laurels –
(And let due emblems of the winter Persephone be displayed throughout
    the grove).

Raise from the flickering world, from the Elysium of the lesser masters,
The Claude Glass and Aeolian Harp, the trophies of his profession;
And pronounce the eulogy of his taste, *virtu* and endurance,
His imagined splendours – palaces, colleges – never accomplished.

And how much courage it takes to live on tirelessness and one's eye,
On the wit which fixes a flicker, an instant, fashions like aspen leaves;
Which says (or withholds) the perfect word, against the claque and
    glimmer of the masquerade,
Amidst whispers that master and valet kissed masked at Carnival,
As did the shepherds of Arcadia in the golden world.

O exile in circles of gentrice without heirs, their distant estates all
    sequestered.

In this removed place, under unaltering midnight,
Raise to his lost renown, arches and fanes of green branches.

V
The Sleeping Laird

Second elegy: to JAS

Dust on the rails of the panelling, bed curtains falling to dust, north wind
    stirring dust as it rises at twilight,
In the solitudes of the rough bounds, his far tower in the foothills, lost in
    the uplands;
The walled garth sifted in leaves, from autumns of geans and the rowan,
Frost cracked slates on the roofs of the turrets,
Walls mossed, spalled flagstones, his armorials smoothed by the rain.

Within: plenishing of shadows, astragal ladders, the passing of starlight,
His chamber of dais deep in forests of tapestry, dim in his mirrors;
The state bed's linen yellowed to the colour of barley,
And weathers and seasons of Scotland lie over his form as he sleeps.

Windblown roses fade on his cheek, his pallor answers the clouds,
As midsummer night scores its gash of brilliance along the northern horizon.
As the wild geese come over in autumn he stirs in his sleep, they cry in the
    language of his dreams,
So his eyelids waver, eyes of matchless sapphire half focus on the rags of
    drapery, the ceiling's stucco emperors, the cornice moulded like snow,
But the flocks cry southwards to silence, dusk comes, his eyes close, and
    night shrouds the coast of the Lothians,
He turns, and the flank of Argyll turns to the dark and the sea.

The branching track at the top of his glen is grown over with bog myrtle
    and rushes,
Showing no traces now of the path rounding the flank of the hill,
By which you could pass to his tower of scoured harling, his garth of crab
    apples and rowans.
But who will ever wake him, since no one can wake him?
Nor till he is woken can we ever be easy or well.
Who might stand at last amidst the dust of his chamber, tears starting in
    their eyes at his handsomeness and our lostness?
Who might lower their lips to his cold, incomparable forehead?

There are those who hold to this day that someone might come, but I fear
    now that nobody will.

VI

The Winter Night

Third and last elegy: *to JBS*

My love, the snow enfolds our policies,
The burn's a thread of shadow under ice;
The track is blocked and frost has stilled the air,
Starlight has made the language of the night
Articulate as crystal. To the south,
Orion's low amidst the frozen trees.
The water to the west's a vacant plain,
And willows sink in ice beyond the island.
Above the runnel by the shadowed bank,
Your ferns have shrunk to frost flowers fixed in rime;
But hellebores grow in your sheltered garden,
Though all of Scotland's motionless in cold.

Only our glasshouse flowers in paradox:
Citrons and olives, jasmine, passion flowers,
Defiant February Hesperides.
You know, in every instance, how to make
So little warmth and light defeat the dark.

In this dead season, box-knots come alive,
Their white formalities loveliest in snow;
Like the still orders of the Dutch parterres,
That bitter night of our first Leiden winter –
The students skating on the steel canals,
Bright-gilded globes and spheres above the spires –
And we by the café window, quiet together.

In the small garden-close against the house,
Our fruit-tree quincunx round the astrolabe
Whose golden arrow's faint in silver light,
Bows leafless branches overborne by snow;
A memory of apple-counties where
We were so often happy in the south,
Amidst the silver rain and the broad trees.

You light snow-lanterns in the greatest cold,
So that one flame, refracted, lights a garden:
This is an emblem of all that you do.

Frost-powdered fields stretch up the slopes beyond,
Glimmer continuous with the plains of stars
Which wheel and turn above us. Midnight comes,
We sleep enfolded by the hills and snow,
At the heart of the garden, of the silent house,
Drifts and the dark piled heavy on the skylights,
We lie together here, will lie together so.

Translations

The echo-madrigal in 'The Keeper of a Troubled House': 'What harmony of the heavens, what golden song?/ *Nothingness./* What transports of the evening, what joys of the morning?/ *If only./* What delights of the morning, crescent at evening?/ *Too late./* The dawn's translucence, the pearl of the Siren of Naples./ *Without hope./* The silent music which is more distinct at twilight./ *Night.*'

The bill posted on the wall in 'Atalanta Fugiens': 'An ingenious young man is sought, fit to copulate with basilisks, and to gratify the desires of the *lamiae*, to blow manticores; steady to look in mirrors, seeing anything but his own face, willing to watch the threshold with drawn silver sword. He must be industrious to count the tears of the *anima mundi*. His reward shall be, when his soul is laid aside, to know the starry flesh of the planetary demons, to go invisible, as free as the crow, above the gibbets and the besieged cities, to pass through the palace of memory leaving no trace in its dust, to live in delight amidst the geometric solids and to go without sorrow amid the burning-glasses and the ruins of Europe.'

'Lamentio umbraticolorum Pastorum': 'The lamentation of the queer shepherds for the death of the Queen of Arcadia./ *Shepherds weep, Nymphs lament/ Alas! The Queen of sad Arcadia is dead./* Bring cypress of the plains and myrtle from the hills/Let the balsam weep perfume, the clouds pearls/ The rains have come, soon the frosts will follow./ *Shepherds weep, Nymphs lament/ Alas! The Queen of sad Arcadia is dead./* The rains have come, soon the frosts will follow/ There are bitter thorns where the strawberries grew/ The trees bow heads already grey./ *Shepherds weep, Nymphs lament/ Alas! The Queen of sad Arcadia is dead./* The trees bow heads already grey/ The rains have come, soon the frosts will follow/ This kingdom once sunlit, once happy, now weeps./ *Shepherds weep, Nymphs lament/ Alas! The Queen of sad Arcadia is dead./* This kingdom once sunlit, once happy, now weeps/ Our festivals are over, our joys have ended/ We offer our pleasures at the funeral pyre of the Queen./ *Shepherds weep, Nymphs lament/ Alas! The Queen of sad Arcadia is dead./* We offer our pleasures at the funeral pyre of the Queen/ Garlands, masks, fans, perfumes/ Flowers of silk and silver, crystal hearts./ *Shepherds weep, Nymphs lament/ Alas! The Queen of sad Arcadia is dead./* Flowers of silk and silver, crystal hearts/ Perfumed and embroidered gloves /Embroidered with flowers like our lost gardens./ *Shepherds weep, Nymphs lament/ Alas! The Queen of sad Arcadia is dead./* Embroidered with flowers like our lost gardens/ The rains muddy the canals, the fountains freeze/ The statues fall, their limbs overgrown with thorns. *Shepherds weep, Nymphs lament/ Alas! The Queen of sad Arcadia is dead.* The statues fall, their limbs overgrown with thorns/ Roses revert to briar, apples to crab-apples/ The groves thicken to a forest./ *Shepherds weep, Nymphs lament/ Alas! The Queen of sad Arcadia is dead./* The groves thicken to a forest./ Where we raise this obelisk to the queen's memory/ And may this marble ever be adorned/ With cypress of the plains and myrtle from the hills.'

The song of the beggars in 'The Praise of Winter': 'Our inheritance is ice and snow/ We were in Eden for so little time. The summer's light hardly lasted/ Now we inherit the night and the winter. And so we pay/ For the apple in Paradise. Snow, ice, crown of thorn/ Prepared as our inheritance. We suffer without complaint/ Praise God for the cold.'